UMBRIA TRAVEL GUIDE 2023

Off-the-Beaten-Path Destinations and Hidden Treasures

REGINA ROSS

Table of Contents

Map of Lake Trasimeno

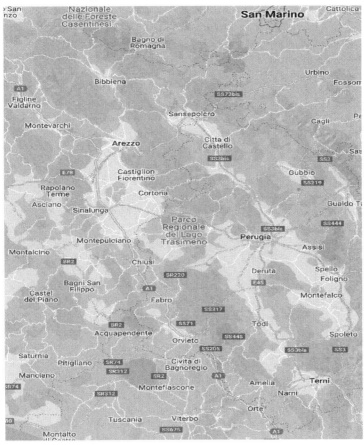

Map of Basilica di Francesco

INTRODUCTION

The Umbria region of Italy is well recognized for its natural beauty and rich culture. It is one of the world's most popular tourist destinations and is located in the country's heart. From its undulating hills to its lively cities, Umbria has something for everyone. Umbria is the ideal destination for your next vacation, whether you want to relax or go on an adventurous adventure.

This travel book will provide you with a comprehensive picture of Umbria. We'll look at the past, current, and cultural highlights of the region. We'll also give you some pointers on how to make the most of your trip. You will be taught the best places to eat, stay, and traverse the city. From historic attractions to cutting-edge cities, Umbria has something for everyone.

Umbria has a long and distinguished history. The region has been inhabited since the dawn of time and was formerly a part of the Etruscan culture. During the Middle Ages, the region was a part of the Papal States before being divided into two provinces. It is today recognized as one of the most historically and culturally significant locations in Italy.

Umbria has some of the most beautiful scenery in the world. From the gently sloping hills of the countryside to the spectacular cliffs of the Adriatic Sea, the area is heaven for outdoor enthusiasts. Aside from sunbathing, guests can walk across the highlands or visit historical ruins.

Umbria has a similarly varied cultural heritage. From a bustling metropolis to little villages, the region is rich in art, culture, and history. Visitors can explore the cathedrals, galleries, and museums, or they can attend a traditional festival. There are also several opportunities to sample regional cuisine and wines.

Finally, there are numerous attractions in Umbria. From the breathtaking vistas of Lake Trasimeno to the wonderful Renaissance architecture of Perugia, the area has something for everyone. Visitors can also engage in outdoor activities such as skiing and rafting.

This guide will help you make the most of your trip to Umbria. We wish you a wonderful journey as you discover the natural beauty and rich culture of this remarkable region.

CHAPTER ONE

About Umbria

Tuscany, Lazio, and Marche are the areas that surround Umbria in central Italy. Despite being one of the country's smallest areas, it is a popular tourist destination due to its natural beauty, cultural heritage, and age-old traditions.

The region is well-known for its picturesque villages, green valleys, and rolling hills. Many of Italy's most famous wines, such as *Orvieto* and *Sagrantino di Montefalco*, are produced in this area, which is densely forested with vineyards and olive groves. Furthermore, the region is known for its spectacular churches, medieval castles, and Roman ruins.

Perugia, the area's heart, is a thriving university town known for its gorgeous architecture, excellent art galleries, and buzzing cafes. Assisi and Gubbio are just two of the many ancient hilltop communities in the vicinity where visitors can wander along cobblestone walks and gaze out at spectacular views.

For real direction from Assisi to Gubbio clink here

Umbria's culture is distinct, incorporating aspects from the Etruscans, Romans, and Renaissance. Throughout the year, numerous festivals and events are held, and traditional cuisine and music remain quite popular. The region is also well-known for religious festivals such as the Holy Cross Procession and the Umbrian Festival of Saint Francis.

Umbria's principal exports are wine and olive oil, and the region's economy is mainly based on agriculture. Tourism is another important component of the economy, with many tourists visiting the area to participate in outdoor activities like hiking, biking, and horseback riding. There are also numerous artisanal firms and workshops in the area that manufacture pottery, textiles, and other crafts.

Overall, Umbria is a lovely region of Italy full of scenic beauty, cultural treasures, and **charming villages**. It is the ideal spot for anyone looking for a true taste of Italy and an amazing experience unrivalled elsewhere.

Charming

History

Umbria is a region in Central Italy located east of Tuscany and south of Marche. Umbria is one of the world's oldest autonomous republics, having been declared a free and independent state by Roman Emperor Augustus in 41 BC.

Umbria has seen its fair share of political instability and has been the site of numerous conflicts over the years. The area was taken over by the Lombards in the eleventh century, and it was afterwards conquered by the Papal States. In the late 18th century, the Kingdom of Italy gained Umbria, which joined the newly united Italian Republic in 1861.

Because of its gorgeous environment and fascinating culture, Umbria is quickly becoming a popular tourist destination. The region is known for its beautiful medieval villages, abundant vineyards, and picturesque undulating hills and valleys. Visitors come to view the area's castles and churches, as well as the numerous outdoor activities offered, including hiking, mountain biking, horseback riding, and hang gliding.

Furthermore, the area is well-recognized for its cuisine, which is based on traditional Italian recipes. Popular recipes include traditional pasta all amatriciana, pork stew with rosemary and garlic, and truffles with wild mushrooms. Umbria produces many of Italy's most well-known wines, including Torgiano, Orvieto, and Sagrantino di Montefalco.

Umbria is a region with a rich and fascinating history, as well as one of the best cultures and cuisines in the country. Travellers looking to experience Italy in all its beauty will find it to be the ideal spot due to its stunning scenery, rich culture, and unique cuisine possibilities.

Torgiano

Geography of Umbria

Umbria, in central Italy, is famous for its lush hills, meandering rivers, and old hill villages. It is surrounded by the regions of Lazio, Marche, and Tuscany. The region is well-known for its beautiful scenery, rich history, and eclectic culture.

The centrally positioned Apennines mountain range has had a profound impact on Umbria's geography. Monte Vettore (2,476 m) is the highest peak in the Sibillini National Park. Another two mountains in the region are Monte Nerone (2,180 m) and Monte Terminillo (2,217 m). The Tiber, Nera, and Chiascio rivers, which have Apennine origins, pass through the area.

Umbria's weather is often pleasant and humid. Winters are mild and damp, whereas summers are hot and dry. The average temperature in July is 25 °C, while it is 5 °C in January. Precipitation falls very evenly throughout the year, about 800mm each year.

Umbria is rich in historical and cultural landmarks. The region is well-known for its numerous churches and castles, such as the

Rocca Maggiore in Spoleto and the Basilica di San Francesco in Assisi. Among the UNESCO World Heritage Sites in the area are Assisi and Monte Sant'Angelo sul Gargano.

Umbria is also well-known for its food. Traditional components include olive oil, cured meats, and truffles. Some of the most well-known wines produced in the area are Torgiano, Sagrantino di Montefalco, and Orvieto Classico.

Umbria is a region rich in culture, history, and natural beauty. With its undulating hills, flowing rivers, and medieval hill towns, as well as its rich culinary and historical attractions, it is a destination that is likely to captivate the senses and thrill the imagination.

CHAPTERS TWO

Where to Go in Umbria

Major cities

Umbria is a region in central Italy that runs from the Tiber River in the west to the Apennine Mountains in the east. Umbria, also known as the *"Green Heart"* of Italy, is home to some of the country's most attractive cities. In 2023, the area is expected to be a bustling tourist destination with a range of attractions, experiences, and activities.

In 2023, the main cities of Umbria are expected to be Perugia, Spoleto, Assisi, Foligno, and Terni. Perugia is Umbria's largest and most populous city, as well as the location of major cultural sites such as the Rocca Paolina, the National Gallery of Umbria, and the Palazzo dei

Priori. The city is also known for its active nightlife, which includes a diverse selection of taverns, restaurants, and nightclubs. Spoleto, on the other hand, is a charming medieval city with cobblestone streets and magnificent landmarks such as the Torre delle Milizie and the Palazzo della Signoria.

One of the most significant religious locations in Italy is Assisi, which is known for the Basilica of St. Francis. The Basilica di Santa Chiara, the Rocca Maggiore, and the Piazza del Comune are among the city's many works of art and architecture. The Duomo di Foligno and the Palazzo Trinci are just two of the many attractions in this city recognized for their vibrant culture. Last but not least, Terni is known for both its natural beauty, like the

Marmore Falls, and its industrial background, particularly the Italsider steelworks.

The number of tourists visiting Umbria is expected to grow even higher in 2023 as the region becomes a more popular tourist destination. In addition to the major city attractions, the area is well-known for its delicious cuisine, breathtaking scenery, and rich history. Furthermore, the area has great transportation links, making it easier to travel to other parts of Italy and Europe. Umbria, with its attractive cities, active environment, and rich culture, will surely become a more popular holiday destination in 2023.

National Park

The National Parks Umbria, one of Italy's largest protected areas, is well recognized for its spectacular natural beauty. The park is widely considered one of the world's most pristine and significant ecosystems, and it is home to a diverse range of unique flora and wildlife. In 2023, the park will celebrate its 50th year of protection, highlighting the area's outstanding biodiversity and importance to the surrounding ecology.

The National Parks Umbria in central Italy includes an area of almost 300,000 hectares. The Italian wolf, Marsican brown bear, Eurasian otter, and golden eagle are just a few of the uncommon and endangered species that live in this huge area. The park contains a variety of tree species, including oak, beech, chestnut, and holm. The park's rigorous laws, which ban activities such as hunting and fishing, protect this incredible diversity of flora and fauna.

The National Parks of Umbria is an important location for scientific research. Scientists from all around the world visit the park to study its ecology and fauna. Experts have recently focused on the park's endangered creatures, such as the Italian wolf, in an effort to maintain their populations. Furthermore, the park's particular ecosystem has become a major draw for ecotourists, who visit to see and appreciate the flora and wildlife.

In 2023, the National Parks Umbria will celebrate 50 years of protection. To mark this occasion, a number of one-of-a-kind activities will be held, including a series of lectures and workshops delivered by specialists from all over the world. The park's management will also launch a series of efforts to raise awareness of the park's unique biodiversity and its importance to the surrounding ecology. Several educational events and programs will be held to help visitors understand the importance of preserving the park's natural beauty.

Basilica di Santa

The National Parks Umbria are one of the world's most important protected areas, and its 50th anniversary of protection in 2023 is a milestone that should be celebrated. The anniversary celebrations will be an excellent chance to highlight the need of protecting and preserving the park's unique biodiversity and its importance to the surrounding environment. With the proper aid and care, the National Parks Umbria will be a source of pride and admiration for many years to come.

Cultural Attractions

Umbria, a region in central Italy, is well-known for its stunning beauty, vibrant culture, and rich history. There are numerous cultural attractions in the area, including medieval monasteries, lively cities, and picturesque hill towns. Umbria offers a diverse selection of activities, from art galleries to ancient monuments.

The Basilica of San Francesco in Assisi is a popular tourist attraction in the area. The narrative of St. Francis, the founder of the Franciscan order, is remembered in this magnificent thirteenth-century basilica. The magnificent interior of the church is open for tourists to explore and see the gorgeous statues and murals. The basilica also offers stunning views of the Umbrian landscape.

Another popular tourist destination in this region is the National Archaeological Museum of Umbria, which is located in Perugia. This museum houses a large collection of ancient Roman and Etruscan artefacts. Visitors can look at antique sculptures and coins while learning about the area's history. The museum is ideal for families because it features a variety of interactive exhibits.

Gubbio has some great churches and architecture. The Basilica di Santa Maria Maggiore is a beautiful cathedral from the 15th century, and the Palazzo dei Consoli is a spectacular palace from the 13th century. Visitors can also walk through the city's medieval passageways and see the Oratorio di San Francesco, a 14th-century chapel.

The majestic church of Orvieto, the Duomo di Orvieto, is well-known. This 14th-century church is embellished with beautiful sculptures, frescoes, and a stunning stained-glass window. Tourists can also explore the city's lovely streets, which are lined with shops, restaurants, and cafes.

Umbria is home to a number of spectacular castles, including the Castello di Montegiove in Spoleto. This majestic stronghold, built in the 13th century, includes impressive towers, courtyards, and walls. The grounds of the castle provide breathtaking views of the surrounding countryside, making it a well-liked tourist attraction.

Umbria is a region rich in history and culture, with attractions for visitors of all ages. This area has something for everyone, from historic sites to breathtaking churches. Whether you wish to learn more about the region's history or admire its stunning scenery, Umbria will provide an amazing experience.

Spellbinding Spello

CHAPTER THREE

Where to Stay in Umbria

Hotel

Umbria is an Italian area famous for its history, natural beauty, and friendliness. Hotels in Umbria offer a vacation experience unlike any other in the world, from lavish five-star hotels to warm family-run inns. In this gorgeous region, visitors may find the right lodging.

The type of lodging is one of the most important considerations when visiting Umbria. Luxury hotels give a high-end experience with amenities such as spas, gourmet dining, and personalized service. These hotels are typically found in larger cities such as Perugia, Terni, and Spoleto. For those seeking a more intimate experience, there are lovely, family-run inns in smaller cities such as Assisi and Orvieto. These inns often offer comfortable lodgings, home-cooked meals, and friendly service.

When renting a hotel in Umbria, it is important to consider the local climate. Because of the possibly hot heat in the summer, an air-conditioned room is required. The surroundings of the hotel should also be considered; many of the top lodgings provide views of the surrounding countryside's lush vineyards and rolling hills. Furthermore, hotels near city centres provide easy access to the area's attractions and culture.

Another important factor to consider while selecting an Umbrian hotel is the degree of service. Many of the area's hotels take great pride in providing a unique experience and excellent customer service. Employees should be friendly and knowledgeable, whether they work at the front desk or as a concierge.

Another important consideration is the cost of lodging in Umbria. Despite the fact that luxury hotels can be rather expensive, there are some mid-range accommodations that provide exceptional value for money. Furthermore, many of the smaller country inns provide discounts for extended stays.

In general, there are numerous hotels to choose from in Umbria. This gorgeous place has something for everyone, whether guests prefer an expensive experience or a cosy, family-run inn. With careful planning and consideration of the different criteria, travellers can select the best hotel for their visit to Umbria.

B&Bs

Umbria is a region in central Italy recognized for its stunning scenery and unique culture. It provides guests with a really one-of-a-kind experience of the area and is home to some of the world's most spectacular Bed and Breakfast (B&B) establishments.

B&Bs in Umbria are often family-run, providing a more personalized and intimate experience than larger hotels and resorts. Many of these B&Bs are located in small towns and villages, giving tourists the opportunity to learn about regional culture and architecture in a relaxed and authentic setting.

B&Bs in Umbria are well-known for their excellent amenities and services. There are several leisure and entertainment options accessible, as well as pleasant lodgings with modern decor and excellent linen. Many B&Bs provide a selection of scrumptious regional cuisine and traditional meals to allow tourists to sample the best of Umbrian food.

Furthermore, the Umbrian B&B staff is highly known for their kindness and hospitality. Many of the owners and employees have been in the sector for several generations, and their local knowledge may be extremely beneficial to guests looking to explore the area.

Last but not least, because of their accessibility, B&Bs in Umbria are a tempting choice for budget-conscious visitors. With rates as low as

€50 per night, visitors to the area can see the sights without breaking the bank.

In summary, B&Bs in Umbria allow guests to explore the region in a unique, inexpensive, and intimate setting. Because of their top-notch amenities, delicious cuisine, and pleasant staff, these locations are excellent alternatives for visitors looking for a truly unique holiday experience.

Camping

Umbria is a growingly popular camping site for visitors wishing to take in the lovely Italian landscape. Umbria, located in the centre of Italy, offers some of the most stunning landscapes in the country, so it's easy to see why it's a favourite with campers. Umbria is a naturalist's paradise, featuring everything from the gently undulating Apennines to the green valleys of the Sibillini Mountains.

When it comes to camping in Umbria, there are several options. For those desiring a more basic experience, the area's campgrounds offer a variety of amenities such as showers and toilets. There are several affluent campgrounds with fully furnished cottages and lodges, as well as upscale campgrounds with private swimming pools and hot tubs, as an option. Whatever type of camping you like, Umbria has something for everyone.

The weather in Umbria is normally pleasant, with warm summers and cool winters. As a result, it's ideal for camping because campers can enjoy the outdoors without worrying about bad weather. The location is ideal for camping during the rainy season because it normally receives a lot of rain during the summer.

Umbria has a lot to offer in terms of entertainment. From kayaking and swimming to hiking and cycling, there is something for everyone. There are also numerous cultural attractions to visit, such as the exquisite medieval cities of Assisi and Orvieto. The abundance of adjacent vineyards, which produce some of the best Italian wine, will also gratify wine connoisseurs.

In addition to all of these activities, camping in Umbria is an excellent way to learn about the region's history and culture. There are numerous Roman and Etruscan ruins in the area, as well as archaeological sites. Campers can also take part in traditional festivals such as the Palio di Siena, an annual horse race held in the town of Siena.

Whether you're looking for a luxurious camping holiday or a demanding outdoor adventure, Umbria has something for everyone. Because of its magnificent beauty, vibrant culture, and diverse choice of activities, Umbria makes camping an unforgettable experience.

Common Travel Phrase you need to know when visit Umbria

	English	Italian
1.	Yes	Si / See
2.	Good morning	Buon giorno
3.	Good afternoon	Buona sera

4.	Good night	Buona notte
5.	Hi / Bye	Ciao!
6.	Good bye	Arrivederci
7.	No	No / Noh
8.	Please	Per favore
9.	Thank you	Grazie
10.	You're welcome	Prego
11.	Cheers!	Salute!
12.	Excuse me	Scusi
13.	Excuse me	Permesso
14.	Do you speak English?	Parla Inglese?
15.	I don't understand	Non capisco
16.	I'm sorry	Mi dispiace
17.	Left	Sinistra

18.	Right	Destra
19.	Straight ahead	Dritto
20.	Forward	Avanti
21.	Back	Dietro
22.	My name is ...	Mi chiamo
23.	What is your name?	Come si chiama?
24.	Pleased to meet you	Piacere
25.	How are you?	Come sta?
26.	Good thank you	Bene grazie
27.	In the morning	Di Mattina
28.	In the afternoon	Di pomeriggio
29.	In the evening	Di Sera
30.	Noon	Mezzogiorno

31.	At what time?	A che ora?
32.	Nine o'clock in the morning	Le nove
33.	Eight o'clock in the evening	Le otto di sera
34.	Monday	Lunedì
35.	Tuesday	Martedì
36.	Wednesday	Mercoledì
37.	Thursday	Giovedì
38.	Friday	Venerdì
39.	Saturday	Sabato
40.	Sunday	Domenica
41.	Today	Oggi
42.	Yesterday	Ieri
43.	Tomorrow	Domani
44.	Can I see the menu please?	Il menu, per favore

45.	What do you recommend?	Che cosa ci consiglia?
46.	I'm allergic to...	Sono allergica/o a...
47.	Gluten / Dairy / Fish	Glutine / Lattecini / Pesce
48.	House wine	Vino della casa
49.	Red / white wine	Vino rosso / bianco
50.	A glass / bottle	Una bicchiere / una bottiglia
51.	Appetizer	Antipasto
52.	First course	Primo
53.	Second course	Secondo
54.	Dessert	Dolci
55.	Two flavors please	Due gusti, per favore
56.	Where's the bathroom?	Dov'è il bagno?
57.	The check (bill) please	Il conto, per favore
58.	Can I pay by card?	Posso pagare con la carta?

59.	When does it open / close?	Quando si apri / chiude?
60.	Two adults / one child	Due adulti / un bambino
61.	One / two ticket's	Un / due biglietto/i _
62.	One senior	Un pensionato
63.	One student	Uno studente
64.	Where is the bag store	cloak room?
65.	Where is... ?	Dov'è...?
66.	Entrance	Entrata
67.	Exit	Uscita
68.	Where is the train station?	Dov'è la stazione?
69.	Where is the bus stop?	Dov'è la fermata
70.	One / two ticket's	Un / due biglietto/
71.	One way	Senso Unico
72.	Return	Ritorno

73.	How much is this?	Quanto costa questo?
74.	OK I'll take it	Va bene, lo prendo
75.	I don't want it	Non lo voglio
76.	Can you ship to...?	Puoi spedire a?
77.	Help!	Aiuto!
78.	I need a doctor	Ho bisogno di un dottore
79.	Call the police	Chiami la polizia
80.	Look out!	Attento!
81.	Go away!	Vai via!

CHAPTER FOUR

What to Eat in Umbria

Local Cuisine

Umbria is an Italian area famous for its wonderful native cuisine. From the savoury Norcia sausages to the creamy cheese of Pienza, the gastronomic delicacies of this region are well-known internationally. This essay will look at the peculiar regional cuisine of Umbria as well as its cultural significance.

Umbrian cuisine is often distinguished by its simplicity and use of local ingredients. This region is known for its fresh meals and locally sourced meats like salami and cured sausages. The Castelluccio di Norcia lentils and Terni farro are only two of the hearty soups and stew prevalent in Umbrian cuisine. Fresh bread, such as Norcia's rosemary focaccia, and cheeses, such as Pecorino di Pienza, is typically used to accompany these dishes.

Umbrian cuisine is noted for its simple yet flavorful dishes, as well as its cultural significance. Because of the region's long winemaking history, numerous local wines, such as the renowned Sagrantino di Montefalco, are utilized in the preparation of the region's meals. Making wine has been passed down through the generations and is being practised now, making it an important part of the local culture.

The Catholic Church has also had a considerable impact on Umbrian cuisine. Assisi's pasta dishes are just one example of the classic food present in numerous eateries throughout Umbria. Because they have been scrupulously preserved and are still enjoyed today, these foods are an important part of the area's cultural past.

Finally, Umbrian cuisine is famous for its flavour and simplicity. The peculiar delicacies of this region, ranging from hearty soups and stews to tasty cured sausages, are a testament to its rich cultural history. The region is particularly well-known for its continued winemaking legacy, which has been passed down through the generations. Umbrian cuisine is a one-of-a-kind and remarkable experience, thanks to the combination of local wines, fresh ingredients, and ancient traditions.

Restaurant

The Umbria area of Italy is famous for its stunning scenery, undulating hills, and delectable cuisine. With its wealth of tiny towns and villages and a vast selection of eateries to choose from, this area is a foodie's heaven. Umbria has a wide range of dining alternatives to suit all preferences, from traditional trattorias and family-owned restaurants to cutting-edge gourmet restaurants.

When it comes to traditional dining venues, Umbria has a plethora of possibilities. One of the most well-known is *La Trattoria del Castello* in *Gubbio*, which serves authentic Umbrian cuisine. Many regional specialities are available here, such as *tagliatelle al tartufo,* which blends homemade pasta with truffle and *Parmigiano-Reggiano* cheese. *Osteria della Ciaia* in Perugia is another well-known restaurant serving regional specialities such as *pappardelle al ragù,* a substantial *ragù* sauce poured over long ribbons of fresh pasta.

For those looking for something a little more modern, Umbria has a lot to offer. *La Corte dei Sapori* in Todi, one of the area's most well-known contemporary cafés, serves unique dishes inspired by regional and seasonal ingredients.

Here, you may enjoy dishes like veal scaloppine with artichokes, an Umbrian classic with a modern touch. *Osteria dei Poeti* in Assisi is another well-known restaurant that serves a variety of dishes influenced by local cuisine.

Todi

In Umbria, no matter what cuisine you prefer, you will find something to your liking. There is something for everyone here, whether you want classic cuisine or something more modern. Umbria is a foodie's paradise, offering everything from little trattorias to gourmet dining venues. Because of its abundance of restaurants, this neighbourhood will undoubtedly satisfy your craving for delectable cuisine.

Gubbio

Wineries

Umbria is an Italian area known for its scenic scenery, old towns, and rich farming. It is also well-known for its wineries, which produce a diverse range of wines that are highly respected for their flavour and quality. Umbria's wineries have a long and storied history, and many are still maintained and owned by families. They make wines that are indicative of the region's terroir, culture, and climate.

Although the wines of Umbria are different, they can be categorized into two categories: *reds* and *whites*. **Sangiovese,** a fruity and structured red wine made from the famous Italian grape, and **Sagrantino di Montefalco**, a full-bodied, tannic red wine made from the indigenous Sagrantino vine, are two Umbrian red wines.

Grechetto and *Trebbiano* are two Umbrian white wines that pair well with shellfish.

The majority of wineries in Umbria are run by families, and several have been producing wine for decades. These wineries range in size from large, modern corporations to small, established farms. Many of the larger vineyards offer tours and tastings so that visitors can learn about the winemaking process and sample some of the region's wines firsthand.

Umbria's climate is ideal for wine production, and the region has a long history of viticulture. Because of the region's rich mineral and organic content, varying topography, and variety of microclimates, winemakers may develop wines with distinct flavours and aromas.

Umbria is home to several noteworthy wineries, and its vineyards are known for producing wines of exceptional quality. For example, *Lungarotti,* one of Umbria's most recognized vineyards, produces a diverse selection of red and white wines that have won numerous awards. *Antinori, Colpetrone, Montefalco, and Arnaldo Caprai* are among the well-known wineries represented.

Umbrian wines are well-known for their flavour and quality, and they have grown in favour among wine enthusiasts worldwide. Umbria is the ideal destination for anyone looking to sample the best Italian winemaking, with a diverse range of red and white wines and a big number of wineries.

CHAPTER FIVE

Transportation in Umbria

Driving

Umbria, a region in central Italy, is a popular vacation destination due to its magnificent beauty, vibrant culture, and delectable cuisine. However, driving in Umbria can be daunting for inexperienced drivers due to its meandering roads, steep mountain crossings, and oftentimes baffling signs. It is critical to understand the principles of driving in Umbria in order to take tourists safely and confidently across the area.

One of the most important aspects of driving in Umbria is understanding traffic laws. The traffic laws in Italy and the rest of the European Union are very similar to those in the United States.

Despite being listed in kilometres per hour, speed limits are basically the same as in the United States. Drivers should always have their license, registration, and proof of insurance with them when turning or changing lanes, and they should use their indicators.

It's also important to comprehend the unique road conditions in Umbria. Because the roads in the region are twisting and usually hilly, they are more challenging to travel on than those in the United States. Drivers should always avoid sharp curves, steep inclines, and other hazards. Drivers should pay extra attention to notice because some routes may be closed due to construction or other causes.

When driving in Umbria, it is critical to be aware of the region's specific cultural practices.

Italians, for example, are said to drive more aggressively than Americans. Drivers should be aware of this and be prepared to respond evasively if necessary. Drivers should also be aware that Italians tend to speed more casually and frequently exceed the speed limits.

Finally, it is critical to be mindful of Umbria's weather possibilities. Thunderstorms and severe rain can hit unexpectedly and without warning due to the region's mountainous geography. Drivers should be prepared for sudden weather changes and take necessary safety precautions, such as slowing down and turning on their headlights.

Travelling by automobile in Umbria can be rewarding and fun in general. Visitors can travel in the area securely and confidently if they follow traffic regulations, are aware of local customs and road conditions, and take proper safety precautions in case of inclement weather.

Public Transportation

Umbria's public transportation infrastructure makes getting about the region simple and inexpensive. Because Umbria is the only area in Italy without a railway infrastructure, the province's public transit relies heavily on its bus network. The bus network includes intercity and intracity lines that connect to neighbouring regions as well as Umbria's major cities and towns. Because they are comfortable, dependable, and reasonably priced, buses are a good choice for travellers who want to explore the area without renting a car.

Umbria has a variety of alternative kinds of transportation in addition to its substantial interstate and intracity bus system. There are various private bus companies that serve the area, as well as numerous boats that connect the coastal villages. If you don't want to rely on public transportation, the area has a variety of automobile rental firms that can provide an inexpensive option to explore.

Umbria is a beautiful region that can be explored without having to drive thanks to its well-developed public transportation system. Thanks to clean and pleasant buses, dependable and safe ferries, and reasonable vehicle rental options, the region may be explored without breaking the bank. Umbria is an ideal location for anyone looking to enjoy the splendours of Italy without having to worry about transportation, thanks to its efficient public transportation system.

Taxis

Taxis play an important role in the transportation system of Umbria, Italy, and are a valuable resource for both inhabitants and tourists. Taxis are available in the majority of the region's major cities and villages, and they provide a quick, convenient, and economical way to get around.

Taxis in Umbria are normally subject to local government supervision, and all drivers must have a license. Drivers must pass many tests in order to receive their license, including a knowledge test and a practical test. All licensed drivers must also keep their vehicles in good working order and have insurance.

Taxis are normally metered and the prices are established by the local government. These prices may vary depending on the time of day, the service given, and the distance travelled. Furthermore, there may be additional charges if you utilize the cab for more than one passenger.

Private taxi services, in addition to metered taxis, are available throughout Umbria. Although they may be more expensive than metered taxis, these services offer a more personalized experience and greater booking and pick-up flexibility. Private cab services can also be more convenient for those who are unfamiliar with the area or who require additional assistance.

Taxis in Umbria are typically reliable and safe, and many of the drivers are familiar with the region and its attractions. It is critical to be aware that certain drivers may be dishonest and attempt to overcharge passengers. To avoid this, it is best to agree on a cost before boarding the cab and to ensure that the meter is turned on. It's also important to be aware of any additional fees, such as those for luggage or late-night travel.

Overall, taxis in Umbria are an important part of the regional transportation network, providing a rapid, easy, and economical way to get around. Travellers can ensure a safe and comfortable journey by following a few easy precautions and being aware of any unexpected fees.

CHAPTER SIX

Shopping in Umbria

Market

Umbria, in central Italy, is known for its large and diversified markets. These markets provide clients with a wide range of fresh and tasty goods and are an excellent source of regional and local products. For the average customer, Umbrian markets offer a diverse range of options, from fruits and vegetables to handmade crafts and artisanal goods.

Perugia's Mercato delle Erbe is one of Umbria's busiest markets. At this twice-weekly market, shoppers can purchase a variety of fresh veggies, cheeses, meats, and other items. It's a great place to meet people and swap stories about life in

Umbria, as well as a nice place to buy fresh local food and other things.

The Mercato di Corso Vannucci in Perugia is another well-known market in Umbria. Customers can buy everything from clothing and jewellery to antiques and handmade things here. This market is a great place to find unique gifts and memories.

Last but not least, the Mercato delle Streghe in Spoleto is a well-known market offering various mystical and magical goods. Because it sells everything from tarot cards and incense to potions and crystals, this market attracts both locals and visitors. It's a fantastic place to find unusual, hard-to-find things that are difficult to find elsewhere.

In addition to these well-known markets, Umbria offers a variety of smaller, more specialised marketplaces. The *Mercato della Terra* in Perugia is a wonderful place to find organic goods and vegetables. Similarly, *Castel Ritaldi's Mercato dei Sapori* is an excellent place to find handcrafted cheeses and meats.

Overall, Umbria is an excellent place to shop for a wide variety of things. Markets in Umbria may provide you with anything you need, from locally produced food to handcrafted goods to more esoteric stuff. Because of its diverse markets, Umbria is an excellent destination for finding one-of-a-kind items. If you ever find yourself in Umbria, be sure to explore the region's numerous markets.

Boutiques

Umbria is a central Italian area known for its beautiful beauty, rich history, and wonderful cuisine. There are also numerous upmarket boutiques that offer a unique shopping experience. Designer apparel, excellent jewellery, and artisan items are all available in Umbrian boutiques.

For those looking for designer goods, Umbria has a number of upmarket clothing boutiques. *Boutique D'Oro,* located in Perugia, is one of the most well-known stores in the area. Customers will find the most recent designer clothing here, including pieces from Prada, Gucci, Versace, and Dolce & Gabbana. Customers can create their own personal style by purchasing custom-tailored clothing at the store.

For those searching for something more unique, there are various businesses that specialize in handcrafted items. These stores sell a variety of handmade goods made by local artisans, such as ceramics, jewellery, and household goods. Two examples are *La Torretta di Deruta*, a ceramic store in *Deruta*, and Jewelry Design, a jewellery store in Terni. Because each of these boutiques sells one-of-a-kind items, they are great for anyone looking for something genuinely unique.

Finally, for those looking for something truly extravagant, there are several boutiques in Umbria that specialize in premium jewellery and timepieces. These boutiques sell a wide range of items from prestigious manufacturers such as Cartier, Rolex, and Bulgari. Gioielli di Perugia and Gioielli di Orvieto, both located in Perugia, are two of the most well-known stores in this category. Customers can select from a wide range of fashionable, high-priced items that will make them stand out.

Finally, Umbrian boutiques offer a unique shopping experience for those looking for a quality, distinctive, and one-of-a-kind item. There are various stores in Umbria that cater to all tastes, whether consumers are looking for high-end timepieces, contemporary clothing, or handmade jewellery. Because of its gorgeous scenery, rich culture, and delectable cuisine, Umbria is a perfect destination for a shopping vacation.

Shopping

Umbria is a region in central Italy known for its beautiful scenery, vibrant culture, and ancient ruins. It is a popular destination for both tourists and locals due to the abundance of retail centres. These shopping centres offer a diverse range of goods and services, from food and entertainment to clothing and electronics. This article will look at some of Umbria's most popular shopping centres and the services they provide.

The *Centro Commerciale Colleverde* in Perugia was Umbria's first shopping centre. This mall has a number of retailers that sell clothing, accessories, and technology. It also has a variety of taverns, restaurants, cafes, a movie theatre, and bowling alleys. Because of its bustling surroundings and nightlife, this shopping centre is particularly popular with young people and couples.

Another retail mall in Umbria is the *Centro Commerciale La Rocca* in Terni. This mall has a number of retailers that sell clothing, accessories, and technology. It also has a variety of taverns, restaurants, cafes, a movie theatre, and bowling alleys. This mall is particularly popular with children and families due to the multitude of activities and entertainment options it offers.

Foligno is home to the Centro *Commerciale della Valle*, one of Umbria's largest shopping areas. This mall has a number of stores providing clothing, accessories, and technology. It also has a movie theater and a bowling alley, as well as a multitude of eateries, cafes, and pubs. This mall is popular with both visitors and locals due to the variety of retailers and entertainment options it offers.

Finally, there's the *Centro Commerciale Galleria,* a well-known *Spoleto* shopping area. This mall has a number of retailers that sell clothing, accessories, and technology. It also has a variety of taverns, restaurants, cafes, a movie theatre, and bowling alleys. This mall is particularly popular with families because it offers a wide range of entertainment and activity options.

Overall, Umbria's retail complexes offer a diverse selection of goods and services to both tourists and locals. These malls are excellent places to go for retail therapy because they include a diverse selection of stores, cafés, cafes, and entertainment opportunities. Whether you want to go shopping or just out for the day,

Conclusion

Umbria's Impact on Italian Culture

Umbria has had a significant impact on Italian culture over the years. It is home to various cultural relics, monuments, and rituals that have shaped the establishment of the country's identity as one of the country's oldest locations. From its culinary heritage to its artistic and architectural treasures, the region has left an indelible mark on the Italian landscape.

Umbria is well-known for its gastronomic legacy, which has played an important part in Italian culture for a long time. *The torta al testo*, a simple yet tasty flatbread made from wheat, water, and salt and traditionally baked on a hot stone, is Umbria's most well-known dish. Typical foods include truffles, olives, and cured meats. The region is home to a number of prominent wineries that create some of Italy's most well-known wines.

Umbria is home to several famous sites and constructions, some of which date back to antiquity. Perugia, the region's capital, is famous for its 13th-century *Fontana Maggiore*, an exquisite fountain, as well as its medieval hilltop defences. The *Rocca Paolina*, a 16th-century castle, and the *Basilica of San Pietro*, a 12th-century Romanesque church, are also noteworthy.

Medieval

Throughout Umbria, there are several traditional festivals and celebrations. The most well-known is the *Calendimaggio*, a May event that includes feasting, singing, and dancing in the cities of *Assisi* and *Spello*. Other popular festivals include the *Sagra dei* Crostini, which celebrates wine and bread, and the *Sagra della Porchetta*, which celebrates roasted pork.

Furthermore, the location has had a great influence on Italian art and architecture. Assisi is home to the Basilica of San Francesco, a masterpiece of Italian Gothic architecture. The *Galleria Nazionale dell'Umbria*, a major art gallery in Perugia, houses works by some of the most well-known local artists, including Raphael and Pinturicchio.

Umbria's cultural heritage is an important part of the country's character and has had a long-lasting influence on Italian history and culture. The gastronomic history, historic sites, customary holidays, and contributions to art and architecture have all created the Italian landscape and cultural identity.

Reasons to Visit Umbria

Umbria, in central Italy, is spectacular and diversified, and it is well renowned for its magnificent scenery, illustrious culture, and wonderful cuisine. Umbria has plenty to offer every type of traveller, whether they are looking for a peaceful escape or a thrilling experience. Here are just a few good reasons to visit this magnificent place.

First and foremost, Umbria is famed for its breathtaking natural beauty. The scenery is stunning, from the gently sloping hills of the countryside to the shimmering blue waters of Lake Trasimeno. Visitors can see the Apennine Mountains' snow-capped peaks, rich vineyards, wildflower fields, and verdant woods. Furthermore, Umbria is home to many attractive towns and villages, such as Orvieto, Assisi, and Gubbio, all of which are well worth visiting.

Umbria is a haven for individuals who love the vast outdoors. There are several opportunities for outdoor activities, including hiking, biking, and exploring the area's numerous caverns, rivers, and waterfalls. Furthermore, Umbria is a superb ski and snowboard destination because it is home to some of Italy's finest ski resorts.

The cultural heritage of the area is important in its attractiveness. Tourists can explore the area's various cathedrals, museums, and other historical buildings in addition to witnessing musical and theatrical performances. Every year, thousands of people visit Umbria for a variety of internationally known events, such as the Sagra dell'Umbria and the Festival of the Red Wine.

Not to mention that Umbria produces some of Italy's most exquisite cuisine. This region has something for everyone, from traditional dishes like minestrone soup and wild boar ragù to regional specialities like porchetta and truffles. Several DOC and DOCG wines from Umbria are among the best in Italy, and the region is well renowned for its excellent wines.

Because of these factors, Umbria is a must-see destination for all visitors. With its amazing natural beauty, recreational activities, cultural attractions, and wonderful cuisine, the area truly has something for everyone. So, why not spend your next trip in Umbria and see everything this beautiful region has to offer?

Printed in Great Britain
by Amazon